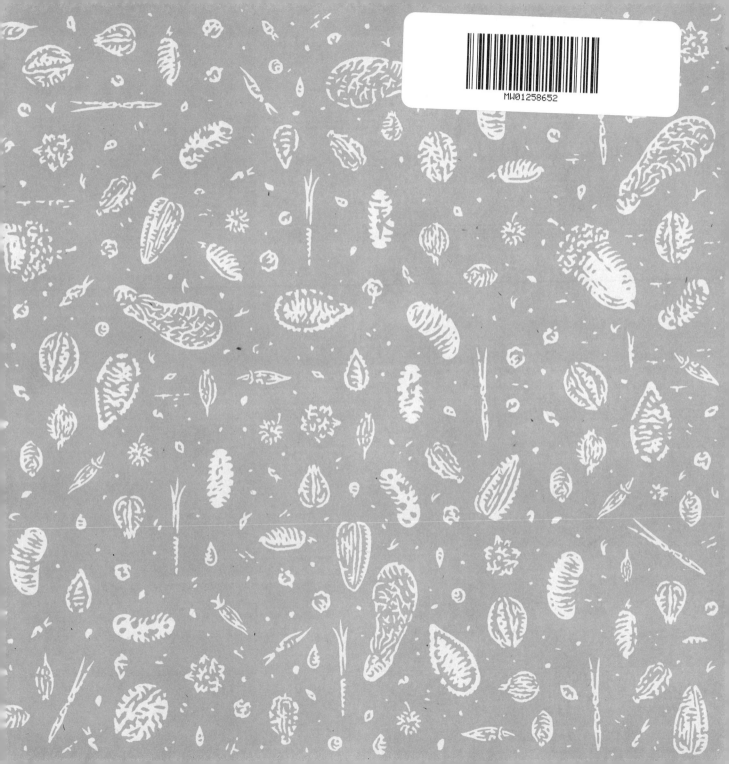

MW01258652

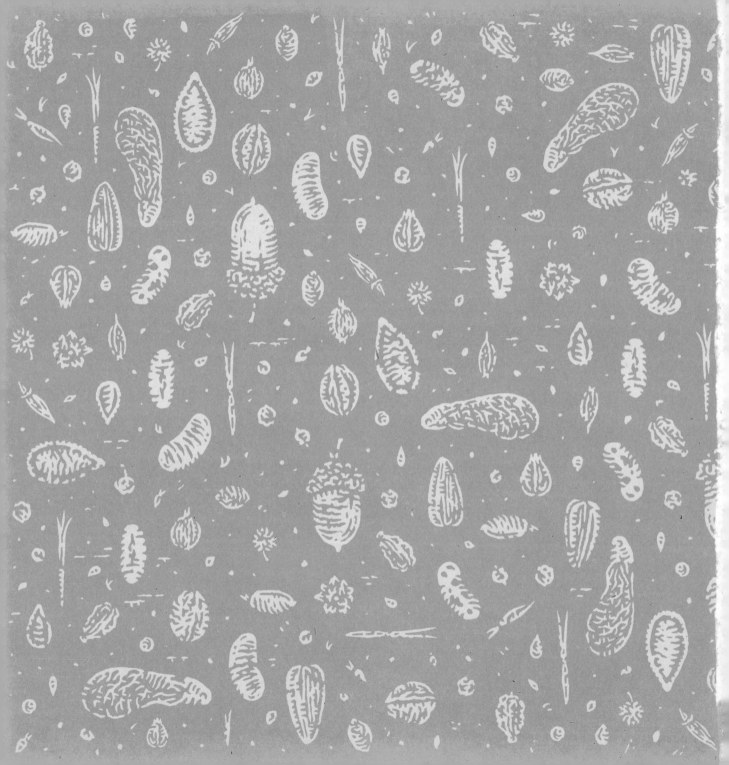

THE SOWER

The Sower

Text copyright © 2022 by Scott James

Illustrations copyright © 2022 by Stephen Crotts

Published by Crossway

      1300 Crescent Street

      Wheaton, Illinois 60187

Cover design: Stephen Crotts

First printing 2022

Printed in China

Scripture quotations are from the ESV® Bible (The Holy Bible, English Standard Version®), copyright © 2001 by Crossway, a publishing ministry of Good News Publishers. Used by permission. All rights reserved.

ISBN: 978-1-4335-7787-1

Library of Congress Cataloging-in-Publication Data

Names: James, Scott, 1979– author. | Crotts, Stephen, illustrator.
Title: The sower / by Scott James ; [illustrations by Stephen Crotts].
Description: Wheaton, Illinois : Crossway, [2022] | Audience: Ages 6–8. |
Summary: "Based on the rich garden motif found throughout the Bible, The Sower
   is the story of God's life-giving work in the world"— Provided by publisher.
Identifiers: LCCN 2021052180 | ISBN 9781433577871 (hardback)
Subjects: CYAC: Christian life—Fiction.
Classification: LCC PZ7.1.J38575 So 2022 | DDC [E]—dc23
LC record available at https://lccn.loc.gov/2021052180

Crossway is a publishing ministry of Good News Publishers.

RRDS		32	31	30	29	28	27	26	25	24	23	22
15	14	13	12	11	10	9	8	7	6	5	4	3	2	1

The SOWER

WRITTEN BY
SCOTT JAMES

ILLUSTRATED BY
STEPHEN CROTTS

CROSSWAY
WHEATON, ILLINOIS

For as the earth brings forth its sprouts,
and as a garden causes what is sown in it to sprout up,
*so the Lord G*OD *will cause righteousness and praise*
to sprout up before all the nations.

ISAIAH 61:11

FOREWORD

When I was a kid, I loved dirt. I used to dig trenches to make little rivers and waterfalls, turn on the hose, and watch till it was all a muddy slush. When I was a kid, I loved trees. I'd sit in a nook of roots to read, or jump into piles of red and yellow leaves. When I was a kid, I loved snow. I loved sunsets and crescent moons. I loved watching the corn sway in the wind, and I loved the sound of thunder when that wind turned into a storm. The Bible tells us that all of creation was made by God and belongs to him. He loves it. I think he's happy when we love it, too—dirt, water, trees, snow, and thunder—because he's like a gardener who delights in our delight. The words and pictures in this book tell a true story about the way God is making the world (including us) new. When you're finished reading it, go outside. Take a good look at this beautiful, broken world, and praise him for what's growing in us and around us. Plant something in the dirt, and watch what God does. The kingdom of heaven, Jesus said, is like a seed. So are you.

Andrew Peterson

Once there was a Voice in the darkness.
Full of light and life, it was the Voice of the Sower.
With a word, he sowed seeds,
and a garden grew.

Roots ran deep into new earth;
branches sprouted fruit, and it was good.
Ever generous, the Sower chose to share his garden.
With a word, he sowed seeds,
and a people grew.

A man and a woman grew strong,
like trees planted beside streams of water.
They loved to hear the Sower's Voice,
for his words brought life.

But another voice tickled their ears,
telling them the Sower was not to be trusted.
So sprouted the first bad fruit:
people doubted the Sower's words.
They wondered if he truly meant good for them.

Hearts turned to darkness and grew hard
as the people stopped listening to the Sower.
They walked away from the source of life
and withered like branches broken from a tree.

The land became filled with people who loved the sound
of their own voice more than the Voice of the Sower.
Sin and sadness grew stronger in the darkness and, with it, fear and shame.
Suffering spread, and the world became like a dry, fruitless land.

But, like a faithful farmer, the Sower continued his creative work.
He knew how to speak into a person's heart, to till it like soil,
to nourish it with light until new life sprouted.
And that's just what he promised to do.

Into a barren land, the Sower sent his powerful Voice with seeds of hope.
He spoke—first through messengers who echoed his love, and then he came himself.
The Sower's Word became flesh and walked among us.
He came to cast seeds and work the soil with his own hands.

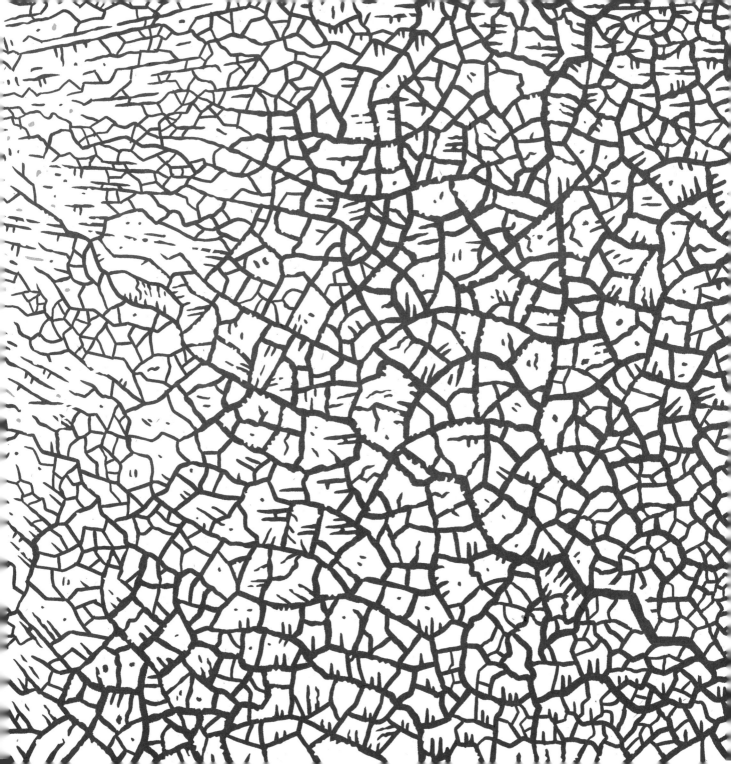

To mend broken people, to make them whole again,
he took their brokenness and made it his own.
He laid himself down, buried like a seed in the ground.

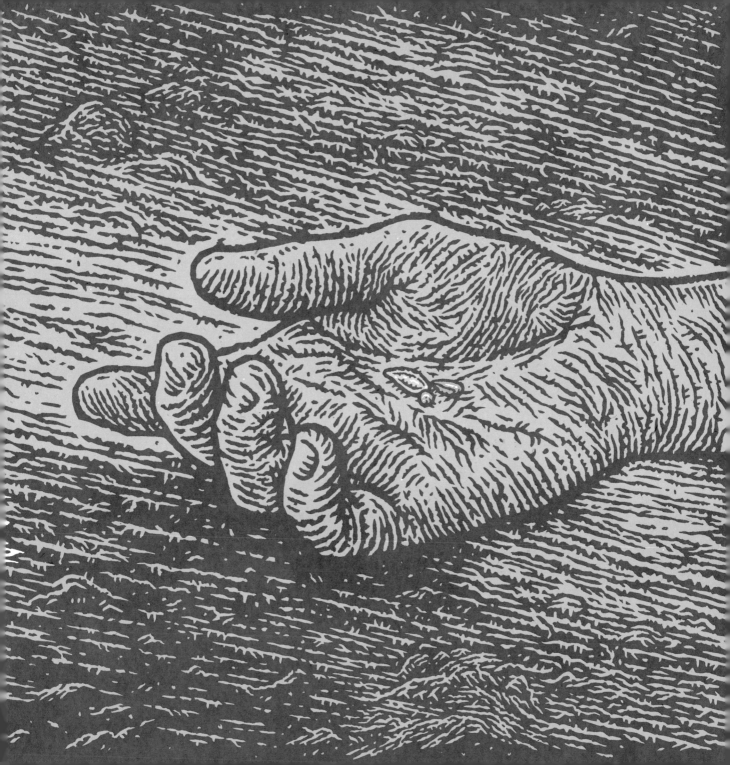

But what does a seed do, once it has been planted?
With a word of power, this Seed rose up into new life,
making a way for his people to rise with him,
fresh branches sprouting from the vine.

And so, the Sower tended his people with care.
He opened their hearts and planted his Voice deep within.
With a word, he sowed seeds.
And miracles grew—faith and hope and love.

His Voice shone down, bringing new life and, with it,
sweet-smelling fruit from those who were once withered.
Some hearts he opened quickly, others took a painful furrowing,
but the Sower's Word brought healing wherever he sent it.

Droughts continued to parch the land,
winter winds laid down their snowy cover wherever they blew,
but those who lived by the Sower's Word stood firm,
gathering strength at the root.

In due season, the Sower's people blossomed
and sent the seed of his Word riding the wind to all corners of the earth.
Redeemed by the Sower, they became sowers too.
They planted, watered, and trusted him to bring new life.

Even now, the Sower calls out with wondrous power,
and the world sings in return.
The garden, once lost, is being remade.
One day we will live with him there,
and as we listen to the sound of his Voice,
we will see him face to face.

The End

For God, who said, "Let light shine out of darkness,"
has shone in our hearts to give the light
of the knowledge of the glory of God
in the face of Jesus Christ.

2 CORINTHIANS 4:6

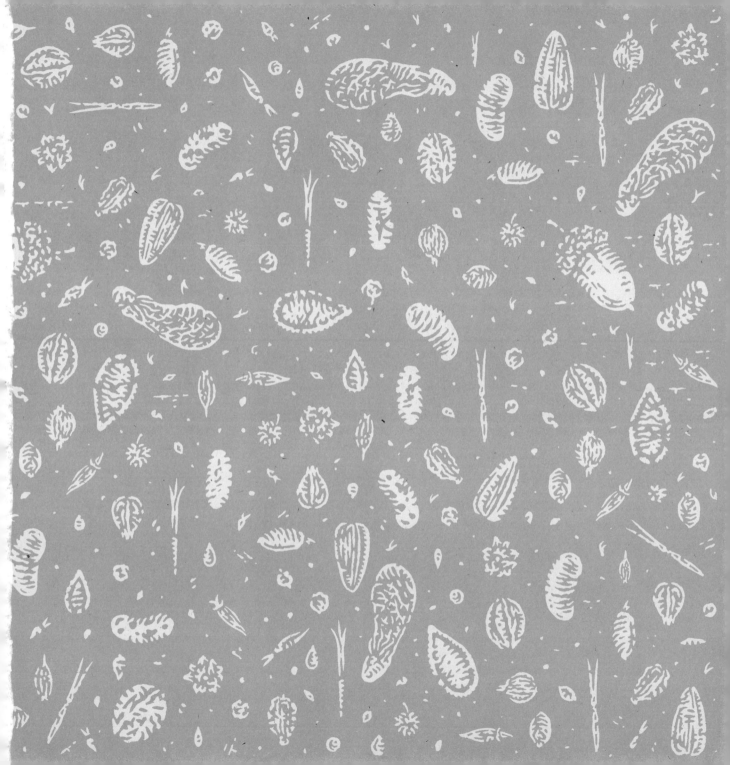

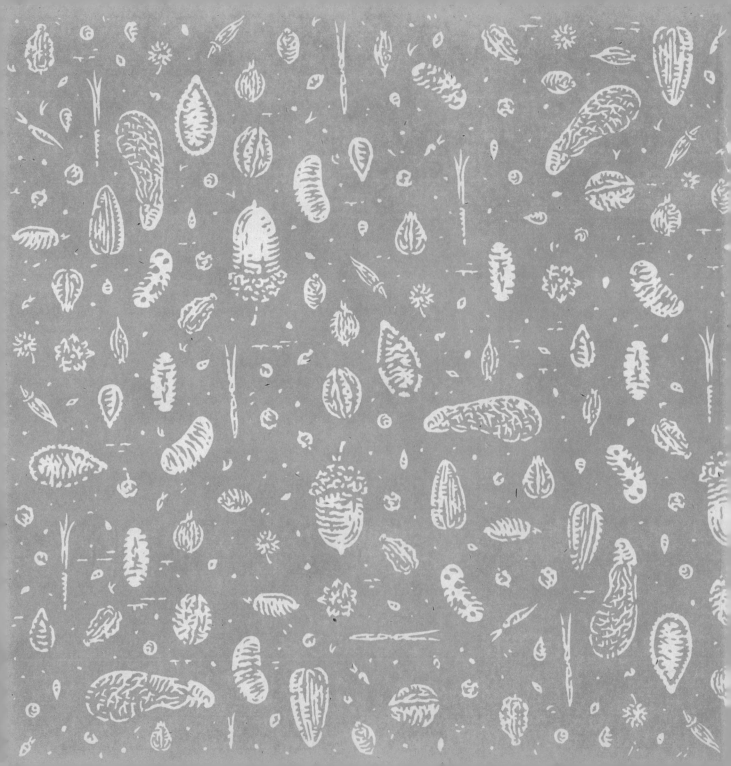